Oscar Wilde's
Guide to
Modern Living

Oscar Wilde's
GUIDE TO
MODERN
LIVING

Edited by

John Calvin Batchelor
and Craig McNeer

DOUBLEDAY

New York   London   Toronto   Sydney   Auckland

PUBLISHED BY DOUBLEDAY
a division of Bantam Doubleday Dell Publishing Group, Inc.
1540 Broadway, New York, New York 10036

DOUBLEDAY and the portrayal of an anchor with a dolphin are trademarks of
Doubleday, a division of
Bantam Doubleday Dell Publishing Group, Inc.

Book design by Maria Carella

Library of Congress Cataloging-in-Publication Data
Wilde, Oscar, 1854–1900.
[Guide to modern living]
Oscar Wilde's guide to modern living / edited by John Calvin Batchelor and
Craig McNeer.
p.   cm.
1. Wilde, Oscar, 1854–1900—Quotations, maxims, etc.   2. Conduct
of life—Quotations, maxims, etc.   I. Batchelor, John Calvin.
II. McNeer, Craig.   III. Title.
PR5812.B3   1996
828'.802—dc20   95-38667
CIP

ISBN 0-385-48179-9

OSCAR FINGAL O'FLAHERTIE WILLS WILDE was born in Dublin in 1854. He was educated at Trinity College, Dublin, and at Magdalen College, Oxford. For fifteen years he enjoyed public acclaim as an author, conversationalist and notable. His showmanship moved him to make a celebrated tour of America. In 1895 in England he was convicted for indecent behavior and jailed two years. He died in Paris in 1900.

Contents

Oscar Wilde's Guide to Modern Living

Advice

I always pass on good advice. It is the only thing to do with it. It is never of any use to oneself.

An Ideal Husband

America

The Americans are certainly great hero-worshippers, and always take heroes from the criminal classes.

OSCAR WILDE

It is a vulgar error to suppose that America was ever discovered. It was merely detected.

OSCAR WILDE

In America, life is one long expectoration.

OSCAR WILDE

American women are wonderfully clever in concealing their parents.

A Woman of No Importance

The youth of America is their oldest tradition. It has been going on now for three hundred years. To hear them talk one would imagine they were in their first childhood. As far as civilization goes they are in their second.

A Woman of No Importance

In America the President reigns for four years, and Journalism governs for ever and ever.

The Soul of Man Under Socialism

All Americans lecture, I believe. I suppose it is something in their climate.

A Woman of No Importance

When good Americans die they go to Paris; when bad Americans die they stay in America.

O<small>SCAR</small> W<small>ILDE</small>

The crude commercialism of America, its materializing spirit, its indifference to the poetical side of things, and its lack of imagination and of high unattainable ideals, are entirely due to that country having adopted for its national hero a man who, according to his own confession, was incapable of telling a lie, and it is not too much to say that the story of George Washington and the cherry-tree has done more harm, and in a shorter space of time, than any other moral tale in the whole of literature.

The Decay of Lying

We have everything in common with America nowadays, except of course, language.

OSCAR WILDE

Art

*A*ll **art is quite useless.**

The Picture of Dorian Gray

We live in an age when men treat art as if it were meant to be a form of autobiography.

<small>O S C A R   W I L D E</small>

Modern pictures are, no doubt, delightful to look at. At least, some of them are. But they are quite impossible to live with; they are too clever, too assertive, too intellectual. Their meaning is too obvious, and their method too clearly defined. One exhausts what they have to say in a very short time, and they become as tedious as one's relations.

<small>O S C A R   W I L D E</small>

The more abstract, the more ideal an art is, the more it reveals to us the temper of its age. If we wish to understand a nation by means of its art, let us look at its architecture or its music.

The Decay of Lying

It is only the unimaginative who ever invents. The true artist is known by the use he makes of what he annexes, and he annexes everything.

OSCAR WILDE

All art is at once surface and symbol. Those who go beneath the surface do so at their peril. Those who read the symbol do so at their peril.

The Picture of Dorian Gray

I hate views, they are only made for bad painters.

OSCAR WILDE

Whenever a community or a powerful section of a community, or a government of any kind, attempts to dictate to the artist what he is to do, Art either entirely vanishes, or becomes stereotyped, or degenerates into a low and ignoble form of craft.

The Soul of Man Under Socialism

A truth in art is that whose contradictory is also true.

The Truth of Masks

The final revelation is that Lying, the telling of beautiful untrue things, is the proper aim of Art.

The Decay of Lying

Art should never try to be popular. The public should try to make itself artistic. There is a very wide difference.

The Soul of Man Under Socialism

The only beautiful things, as somebody once said, are the things that do not concern us. As long as a thing is useful or necessary to us, or affects us in any way, either for pain or for pleasure, or appeals strongly to our sympathies, or is a vital part of the environment in which we live, it is outside the proper sphere of art. To art's subject-matter we should be more or less indifferent.

The Decay of Lying

To reveal art and conceal the artist is art's aim.

The Picture of Dorian Gray

The fact is, the public make use of the classics of a country as a means of checking the progress of Art. They degrade the classics into authorities.

The Soul of Man Under Socialism

When they say a work is grossly unintelligible, they mean that the artist has said or made a beautiful thing that is new; when they describe a work as grossly immoral, they mean that the artist has said or made a beautiful thing that is true. The former expression has reference to style; the latter to subject-matter. But they probably use the words very vaguely, as an ordinary mob will use ready-made paving-stones.

The Soul of Man Under Socialism

The proper school to learn art in is not Life but Art.

The Decay of Lying

The Impossible in art is anything that has happened in real life.

Oscar Wilde

What Art really reveals to us is Nature's lack of design, her curious crudities, her extraordinary monotony, her absolutely unfinished condition. Nature has good intentions, of course, but, as Aristotle once said, she cannot carry them out. When I look at a landscape I cannot help seeing all its defects.

The Decay of Lying

No artist has ethical sympathies. An ethical sympathy in an artist is an unpardonable mannerism of style.

The Picture of Dorian Gray

A great artist invents a type, and Life tries to copy it, to reproduce it in a popular form, like an enterprising publisher.

The Decay of Lying

It is the spectator, and not life, that art really mirrors.

The Picture of Dorian Gray

No great artist ever sees things as they really are. If he did, he would cease to be an artist.

The Decay of Lying

We can forgive a man for making a useful thing as long as he does not admire it. The only excuse for making a useless thing is that one admires it intensely.

The Picture of Dorian Gray

All bad art comes from returning to Life and Nature, and elevating them into ideals.

The Decay of Lying

The Atlantic

*ℐ am not exactly
pleased with the
Atlantic; it is not so
majestic as I expected.*

Oscar Wilde

Beauty reveals everything, because it expresses nothing.

The Critic as Artist

Most women are so artificial they have no sense of Art. Most men are so natural that they have no sense of Beauty.

OSCAR WILDE

All beautiful things belong to the same age.

Pen, Pencil and Poison

I have found that all ugly things are made by those who strive to make something beautiful, and that all beautiful things are made by those who strive to make something useful.

OSCAR WILDE

Comedy

The world has always laughed at its own tragedies, that being the only way in which it has been able to bear them. And that, consequently, whatever the world has treated seriously belongs to the comedy side of things.

A Woman of No Importance

The Critic

Criticism is the highest form of autobiography.

Oscar Wilde

Praise makes me humble, but when I am abused I know I have touched the stars.

Oscar Wilde

As a method Realism is a complete failure, and the two things that every artist should avoid are modernity of form and modernity of subject-matter.

The Decay of Lying

When critics disagree the artist is in accord with himself.

The Picture of Dorian Gray

When man acts he is a puppet. When he describes he is a poet.

The Critic as Artist

Popularity is the one insult I have never suffered.

The Duchess of Padua

The critic is he who can translate into another manner or a new material his impression of beautiful things. The highest, as the lowest, form of criticism is a mode of autobiography.

The Picture of Dorian Gray

The primary aim of the critic is to see the object as it really is not.

Oscar Wilde

Action! What is action? It dies at the moment of its energy. It is a base concession to fact. The world is made by the singer for the dreamer.

The Critic as Artist

Deathbed

My wallpaper and I are fighting a duel to the death. One or the other of us has to go.

<small>OSCAR WILDE</small>

Dickens

One must have a heart of stone to read the death of Little Nell without laughing.

Oscar Wilde

Dullness

*D**ullness is the coming of age of seriousness.***

Phrases and Philosophies for the Use of the Young

Don't let us discuss anything solemnly. I am but too conscious of the fact that we are born in an age when only the dull are treated seriously, and I live in terror of being misunderstood.

The Critic as Artist

Eating

After a good dinner one can forgive anybody, even one's own relations.

A Woman of No Importance

When I am in trouble, eating is the only thing that consoles me. Indeed, when I am in really great trouble, as any one who knows me intimately will tell you, I refuse everything except food and drink.

At the present moment I am eating muffins because I am unhappy. Besides, I am particularly fond of muffins.

The Importance of Being Earnest

Only dull people are brilliant at breakfast.

An Ideal Husband

I can't eat muffins in an agitated manner. The butter would probably get on my cuffs. One should always eat muffins quite calmly. It is the only way to eat them.

The Importance of Being Earnest

Education

Education is an admirable thing, but it is well to remember from time to time that nothing that is worth knowing can be taught.

The Critic as Artist

All thought is immoral. Its very essence is destruction. If you think of anything, you kill it. Nothing survives being thought of.

A Woman of No Importance

The mind of a thoroughly well-informed man is a dreadful thing. It is like a bric-à-brac shop, all monsters and dust, with everything priced above its proper value.

The Picture of Dorian Gray

Don't degrade me into the position of giving you useful information.

The Critic as Artist

The man who is so occupied in trying to educate others has never had any time to educate himself.

OSCAR WILDE

In examinations the foolish ask questions that the wise cannot answer.

Phrases and Philosophies for the Use of the Young

He has never written a single book, so you can imagine how much he knows.

The Importance of Being Earnest

The fact is that the public have an insatiable curiosity to know everything, except what is worth knowing.

The Soul of Man Under Socialism

It is a very sad thing that nowadays there is so little useless information.

OSCAR WILDE

I am afraid that we are beginning to be over-educated; at least everybody who is incapable of learning has taken to teaching—that is really what our enthusiasm for education has come to.

The Decay of Lying

I do not approve of anything that tampers with natural ignorance. Ignorance is like a delicate exotic fruit; touch it and the bloom is gone.

The Importance of Being Earnest

Family

Children begin by loving their parents. After a time they judge them. Rarely, if ever, do they forgive them.

A Woman of No Importance

Fathers should be neither seen nor heard. That is the only proper basis for family life. Mothers are different. Mothers are darlings.

An Ideal Husband

To lose one parent, may be regarded as a misfortune; to lose both looks like carelessness.

The Importance of Being Earnest

What does it matter whether a man has ever had a father and mother or not? Mothers, of course, are all right. They pay a chap's bills and don't bother him. But fathers bother a chap and never pay his bills. I don't know a single chap at the club who speaks to his father.

The Importance of Being Earnest

Families are so mixed nowadays. Indeed, as a rule, everybody turns out to be somebody else.

An Ideal Husband

Fashion

Fashion is what one wears oneself. What is unfashionable is what other people wear.

An Ideal Husband

One should never give a woman anything that she can't wear in the evening.

An Ideal Husband

One should either be a work of art, or wear a work of art.

Phrases and Philosophies for the Use of the Young

The only way to atone for being occasionally a little over-dressed is by being always absolutely over-educated.

Phrases and Philosophies for the Use of the Young

Greek dress was in its essence inartistic. Nothing should reveal the body but the body.

Phrases and Philosophies for the Use of the Young

He has nothing, but he looks everything. What more can one desire?

The Importance of Being Earnest

Fashion is a contrived epidemic.

Oscar Wilde

A fashion is merely a form of ugliness so unbearable that we are compelled to alter it every six months.

Oscar Wilde

Fin de Siècle

You are little more than a mere sentimentalist. A type I have but little respect for, common though it is at the end of this, as of every century.

The Importance of Being Earnest

Friendship

Anyone can sympathize with the sufferings of a friend, but it requires a very fine nature to sympathize with a friend's success.

OSCAR WILDE

Friendship is far more tragic than love. It lasts longer.

OSCAR WILDE

It is always painful to part from people whom one has known for a very brief space of time. The absence of old friends one can endure with equanimity. But even a momentary separation from any one to whom one has just been introduced is almost unbearable.

The Importance of Being Earnest

Genius

I have put only my talent into my works. I have put all my genius into my life.

OSCAR WILDE

I have nothing to declare except my genius.

OSCAR WILDE

Not being a genius, he had no enemies.

Lord Arthur Savile's Crime

Gentlemen

Exercise! Good God! No gentleman ever takes exercise. You don't seem to understand what a gentleman is.

The Importance of Being Earnest

My duty as a gentleman has never interfered with my pleasures in the smallest degree.

The Importance of Being Earnest

A gentleman never looks out of the window.

OSCAR WILDE

It is a very ungentlemanly thing to read a private cigarette case.

The Importance of Being Earnest

Examinations are of no value whatsoever. If a man is a gentleman, he knows quite enough, and if he is not a gentleman, whatever he knows is bad for him.

A Woman of No Importance

Gossip

There is only one thing worse in the world than being talked about and that is not being talked about.

OSCAR WILDE

Guidance

Moderation is a fatal thing. Nothing succeeds like excess.

A Woman of No Importance

All influence is bad, but a good influence is the worst in the world.

A Woman of No Importance

Oh, don't use big words. They mean so little.

An Ideal Husband

It is always worth while asking a question, though it is not always worth while answering one.

An Ideal Husband

Nothing looks so like innocence as an indiscretion.

Lady Windermere's Fan

One should always be a little improbable.

Phrases and Philosophies for the Use of the Young

A man cannot be too careful in the choice of his enemies.

Oscar Wilde

One should never listen. To listen is a sign of indifference to one's hearers.

Oscar Wilde

Resist everything except temptation.

Lady Windermere's Fan

Health

Exercise! The only possible exercise is to talk, not to walk.

OSCAR WILDE

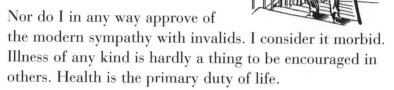

Nor do I in any way approve of the modern sympathy with invalids. I consider it morbid. Illness of any kind is hardly a thing to be encouraged in others. Health is the primary duty of life.

The Importance of Being Earnest

Not ill, only tired. The fact is, I picked a primrose in the wood yesterday and it was so ill, I have been sitting up with it all night.

OSCAR WILDE

The doctor is fighting for a theory. The man is fighting for his life.

OSCAR WILDE

History

Gossip is charming! History is merely gossip. But scandal is gossip made tedious by morality.

Lady Windermere's Fan

Facts are not merely finding a footing-place in history, but they are usurping the domain of Fancy, and have invaded the kingdom of Romance. Their chilling touch is over everything. They are vulgarizing mankind.

The Decay of Lying

The ages live in history through their anachronisms.

Phrases and Philosophies for the Use of the Young

History never repeats itself. The historians repeat each other. There is a wide difference.

OSCAR WILDE

The one duty we owe to history is to rewrite it.

The Critic as Artist

As one reads history, not in the expurgated editions written for schoolboys and passmen, but in the original authorities of each time, one is absolutely sickened, not by the crimes that the wicked have committed, but by the punishments that the good have inflicted; and a community is infinitely more brutalized by the habitual employment of punishment than it is by the occasional occurrence of crime.

The Soul of Man Under Socialism

I know that there are many historians, or at least writers on historical subjects, who still think it necessary to apply moral judgments to history, and who distribute their praise or blame with the solemn complacency of a successful schoolmaster. This, however, is a foolish habit and merely shows that the moral instinct can be brought to such a pitch of perfection that it will make its appearance wherever it is not required. Nobody with the true historical sense ever dreams of blaming Nero, or scolding Tiberius, or censuring Caesar Borgia. These personages have become like the puppets of a play. They may fill us with terror, or horror, or wonder, but they do not harm us. They are not in immediate relation to us. We have nothing to fear from them. They have passed into the sphere of art and science and neither art nor science knows anything of moral approval or disapproval.

Pen, Pencil and Poison

Langtry

I would rather have discovered Mrs. Langtry than have discovered America.

OSCAR WILDE

Life

Nothing should be out of the reach of hope. Life is a hope.

A Woman of No Importance

Life is far too important a thing ever to talk seriously about it.

Lady Windermere's Fan

The first duty in life is to be as artificial as possible. What the second duty is no one has as yet discovered.

Phrases and Philosophies for the Use of the Young

The secret of life is to appreciate the pleasure of being terribly, terribly deceived.

A Woman of No Importance

Pleasure is the only thing one should live for. Nothing ages like happiness.

Phrases and Philosophies for the Use of the Young

And as for Life, she is the solvent that breaks up Art, the enemy that lays waste her house.

The Decay of Lying

Life is simply a *mauvais quart d'heure* made up of exquisite moments.

A Woman of No Importance

You must not find symbols in everything you see. It makes life impossible.

Salomé

Love

Where there is no extravagance there is no love, and where there is no love there is no understanding.

OSCAR WILDE

When one is in love one begins by deceiving oneself. And one ends by deceiving others. That is what the world calls a romance.

A Woman of No Importance

Poets know how useful passion is for publication. Nowadays a broken heart will run to many editions.

OSCAR WILDE

The worst of having a romance is that it leaves one so unromantic.

OSCAR WILDE

Nothing spoils a romance so much as a sense of humor in the woman. Or the want of it in the man.

A Woman of No Importance

Men always want to be a woman's first love. That is their clumsy vanity. We women have a more subtle instinct about things. What we like is to be a man's last romance.

A Woman of No Importance

I suppose that when a man has once loved a woman, he will do anything for her, except continue to love her?

An Ideal Husband

The only difference between a caprice and a lifelong passion is that the caprice lasts a little longer.

OSCAR WILDE

A *grande passion* is the privilege of people who have nothing to do. That is the one use of the idle classes of a country.

The Picture of Dorian Gray

One should always be in love. That is the reason one should never marry.

A Woman of No Importance

I really don't see anything romantic in proposing. It is very romantic to be in love. But there is nothing romantic about a definite proposal. Why, one may be accepted. One usually is, I believe. Then the excitement is all over. The very essence of romance is uncertainty. If ever I get married, I'll certainly try to forget the fact.

The Importance of Being Earnest

Faithfulness is to the emotional life what consistency is to the life of the intellect—simply a confession of failure.

OSCAR WILDE

It is difficult not to be unjust to what one loves.

The Critic as Artist

Marriage

M̶en marry because they are tired; women because they are curious. Both are disappointed.

A Woman of No Importance

The proper basis for marriage is mutual misunderstanding.

Lord Arthur Savile's Crime

The happiness of a married man depends on the people he has not married.

OSCAR WILDE

There is only one real tragedy in a woman's life. The fact that her past is always her lover, and her future invariably her husband.

An Ideal Husband

I think to elope is cowardly. It's running away from danger.

A Woman of No Importance

So much marriage is certainly not becoming. Twenty years of romance make a woman look like a ruin; but twenty years of marriage make her something like a public building.

A Woman of No Importance

Divorces are made in Heaven.

The Importance of Being Earnest

It's perfectly scandalous the amount of bachelors who are going about society. There should be a law passed to compel them all to marry within twelve months.

A Woman of No Importance

The amount of women who flirt with their own husbands is perfectly scandalous. It looks so bad. It is simply washing one's clean linen in public.

The Importance of Being Earnest

Nothing ages a woman so rapidly as having married the general rule.

An Ideal Husband

I have always been of opinion that a man who desires to get married should know either everything or nothing.

The Importance of Being Earnest

It is the growth of the moral sense of women that makes marriage such a hopeless, one-sided institution.

An Ideal Husband

No married man is ever attractive except to his wife.

The Importance of Being Earnest

A man can be happy with any woman, as long as he does not marry her.

Oscar Wilde

Oh, no good chap makes a good husband. If a chap makes a good husband there must have been something rather peculiar about him when he was a bachelor. To be a good husband requires considerable practice.

The Importance of Being Earnest

In married life three is company, two is none.

Oscar Wilde

To speak frankly, I am not in favor of long engagements. They give people the opportunity of finding out each other's character before marriage, which I think is never advisable.

The Importance of Being Earnest

One should always be in love. That is the reason one should never marry.

Oscar Wilde

It would hardly have been a really serious engagement if it hadn't been broken off at least once.

The Importance of Being Earnest

Men

All women become like their mothers. That is their tragedy. No man does. That is his.

A Woman of No Importance

Men become old, but they never become good.

Lady Windermere's Fan

By persistently remaining single, a man converts himself into a permanent public temptation. Men should be more careful; this very celibacy leads weaker vessels astray.

The Importance of Being Earnest

All men are married women's property. That is the only true definition of what married women's property really is.

A Woman of No Importance

When men give up saying what is charming, they give up thinking what is charming.

Lady Windermere's Fan

Oh, the Ideal Man would talk to us as if we were goddesses and treat us as if we were children. He should refuse all our serious requests, and gratify every one of our whims. He should encourage us to have caprices, and forbid us to have missions. He should always say much more than he means, and always mean much more than he says. If we ask him a question about anything, he should give us an answer all about ourselves. He should invariably praise us for whatever qualities he knows we haven't got. But he should be pitiless, quite pitiless, in reproaching us for the virtues that we have never dreamed of possessing. He should never believe that we know the use of useful things. That would be unforgivable. But he should shower on us everything we don't want.

A Woman of No Importance

I will predict, accurately, all human behavior except that which governs the human heart. Man is constant in his infidelity and woman puts him to shame because she is, by nature, fickle.

OSCAR WILDE

Rich bachelors should be heavily taxed. It is not fair that some men should be happier than others.

OSCAR WILDE

All that I have noticed is that men are horribly tedious when they are good husbands, and abominably conceited when they are not.

A Woman of No Importance

The higher education of men is what I should like to see. Men need it so sadly.

An Ideal Husband

Young men want to be faithful, and are not: old men want to be faithless, and cannot.

The Picture of Dorian Gray

Men who are trying to do something for the world, are always insufferable. When the world has done something for them, they are charming.

OSCAR WILDE

The Modern

Nothing is so dangerous as being too modern. One is apt to grow old-fashioned quite suddenly.

An Ideal Husband

The truth is rarely pure and never simple. Modern life would be very tedious if it were either, and modern literature a complete impossibility!

The Importance of Being Earnest

To be Greek one should have no clothes: to be medieval one should have no body: to be modern one should have no soul.

Oscar Wilde

Modern wallpaper is so bad that a boy brought up under its influence could allege it as a justification for turning to a life of crime.

Oscar Wilde

In modern life nothing produces such an effect as a good platitude. It makes the whole world kin.

An Ideal Husband

It is absurd to have a hard and fast rule about what one should read and what one shouldn't. More than half of modern culture depends on what one shouldn't read.

The Importance of Being Earnest

Civilizations continue because people hate them. A modern city is the exact opposite of what everyone wants.

OSCAR WILDE

Money

It is only by not paying one's bills that one can hope to live in the memory of the commercial classes.

Phrases and Philosophies for the Use of the Young

Industry is the root of all ugliness.

Phrases and Philosophies for the Use of the Young

Every man of ambition has to fight his century with its own weapons. What this century worships is wealth. The God of this century is wealth. To succeed one must have wealth. At all costs one must have wealth.

OSCAR WILDE

In modern life margin is everything.

Lady Windermere's Fan

What is a cynic? A man who knows the price of everything and the value of nothing.

Lady Windermere's Fan

Property is really a nuisance. Some years ago people went about the country saying that property has duties. They said it so often and so tediously that, at last, the Church has begun to say it. One hears it from every pulpit. It is perfectly true. Property not merely has duties, but has so many duties that its possession to any large extent is a bore. It involves endless claims upon one, endless attention to business, endless bother. If property had simply pleasures, we could stand it; but its duties make it unbearable. In the interest of the rich we must get rid of it.

The Soul of Man Under Socialism

Ambition is the last refuge of the failure.

Phrases and Philosophies for the Use of the Young

Time is waste of money.

Phrases and Philosophies for the Use of the Young

What between the duties expected of one during one's lifetime, and the duties exacted from one after one's death, land has ceased to be either a profit or a pleasure. It gives one position, and prevents one from keeping it up. That's all that can be said about land.

The Importance of Being Earnest

Morality

Intellectual generalities are always interesting, but generalities in morals mean absolutely nothing.

A Woman of No Importance

Manners before morals!

Lady Windermere's Fan

Morality is simply the attitude we adopt towards people whom we personally dislike.

An Ideal Husband

The only difference between the saint and the sinner is that every saint has a past, and every sinner has a future.

A Woman of No Importance

Any preoccupation with ideas of what is right or wrong in conduct shows an arrested intellectual development.

Phrases and Philosophies for the Use of the Young

If the lower orders don't set us a good example, what on earth is the use of them? They seem, as a class, to have absolutely no sense of moral responsibility.

The Importance of Being Earnest

The moral life of man forms part of the subject-matter of the artist, but the morality of art consists in the perfect use of an imperfect medium. No artist desires to prove anything. Even things that are true can be proved.

The Picture of Dorian Gray

It requires merely physical courage to sacrifice oneself. To sacrifice others moral courage is necessary.

The Importance of Being Earnest

Women represent the triumph of matter over mind—just as men represent the triumph of mind over morals.

A Woman of No Importance

The basis of every scandal is an absolutely immoral certainty.

A Woman of No Importance

Murder

I should fancy, however, murder is always a mistake. One should never do anything that one cannot talk about after dinner.

The Picture of Dorian Gray

Nature

Let us go and lie on the grass and smoke cigarettes and enjoy Nature.

The Decay of Lying

Nature is so uncomfortable. Grass is hard and lumpy and damp, and full of dreadful black insects.

The Decay of Lying

If Nature had been comfortable, mankind would never have invented architecture, and I prefer houses to the open air.

The Decay of Lying

Like most artificial people, he had a great love of nature.

Pen, Pencil and Poison

Nature is always behind the age.

The Decay of Lying

Nobody of any real culture, for instance, ever talks nowadays about the beauty of a sunset. Sunsets are quite old-fashioned. They belong to the time when Turner was the last note in art. To admire them is a distinct sign of provincialism of temperament.

The Decay of Lying

Niagara Falls

Every American bride is taken there, and the sight of this stupendous waterfall must be one of the earliest, if not one of the keenest, disappointments of American life.

Oscar Wilde

Novel

In old days books were written by men of letters and read by the public. Nowadays books are written by the public and read by nobody.

Oscar Wilde

Anybody can write a three-volumed novel. It merely requires a complete ignorance of both life and literature.

The Critic as Artist

To invent anything at all is an act of sheer genius, and, in a commercial age like ours, shows considerable physical courage— Few of our modern novelists ever dare to invent a single thing. It is an open secret that they don't know how to do it.

The Importance of Being Earnest

I am never disappointed in literary men. I think they are perfectly charming. It is their works I find so disappointing.

Oscar Wilde

In reading a purely modern novel, we have rarely any artistic pleasure in re-reading it. And this is perhaps the best rough test of what is literature and what is not. If one cannot enjoy reading a book over and over again, there is no use reading it at all.

The Decay of Lying

The one thing that the public dislike is novelty.

The Soul of Man Under Socialism

Mr. Henry James writes fiction as if it were a painful duty, and wastes upon mean motives and imperceptible "points of view" his neat literary style, his felicitous phrases, his swift and caustic satire.

The Decay of Lying

The ancient historians gave us delightful fiction in the form of fact; the modern novelist presents us with dull facts under the guise of fiction.

The Decay of Lying

The good ended happily, and the bad unhappily. That is what Fiction means.

The Importance of Being Earnest

The public like to insult poets because they are individual, but once they have insulted them, they leave them alone. In the case of the novel and the drama, arts in which the public do take an interest, the result of the exercise of popular authority has been absolutely ridiculous.

The Soul of Man Under Socialism

As for that great and daily increasing school of novelists for whom the sun always rises in the East-End, the only thing that can be said about them is that they find life crude, and leave it raw.

The Decay of Lying

There is no such thing as a moral or an immoral book. Books are well written, or badly written. That is all.

The Picture of Dorian Gray

The only real people are the people who never existed, and if a novelist is base enough to go to life for his personages

he should at least pretend that they are creations, and not
boast of them as copies.

The Decay of Lying

The justification of a character in a novel is not that other
persons are what they are, but that the author is what he
is. Otherwise the novel is not a work of art.

The Decay of Lying

The Nihilist, that strange martyr who has no faith, who
goes to the stake without enthusiasm, and dies for what he
does not believe in, is a purely literary product. He was
invented by Turgenev, and completed by Dostoyevsky.
Robespierre came out of the pages of Rousseau as surely as
the People's Palace rose out of the debris of a novel.
Literature always anticipates life. It does not copy it, but
molds it to its purpose.

The Decay of Lying

Romantic surroundings are the worst surroundings
possible for a romantic writer.

Oscar Wilde

Observations

To disagree with three fourths of the public on all points is one of the first elements of sanity.

OSCAR WILDE

Experience is the name every one gives to their mistakes.

Lady Windermere's Fan

Nothing that actually occurs is of the smallest importance.

Phrases and Philosophies for the Use of the Young

The more one analyzes people, the more all reasons for analysis disappear. Sooner or later one comes to that dreadful universal thing called human nature. Indeed, as anyone who has ever worked among the poor knows only too well, the brotherhood of man is no mere poet's dream, it is a most depressing and humiliating reality; and if a writer insists upon analyzing the upper classes, he might just as well write of match-girls and costermongers at once.

The Decay of Lying

There is a fatality about all good resolutions. They are invariably made too soon.

Phrases and Philosophies for the Use of the Young

After playing Chopin, I feel as if I had been weeping over sins that I had never committed, and mourning over tragedies that were not my own.

The Critic as Artist

To have been well brought up is a great drawback nowadays. It shuts one out from so much.

A Woman of No Importance

I adore simple pleasures. They are the last refuge of the complex.

A Woman of No Importance

Questions are never indiscreet. Answers sometimes are.

An Ideal Husband

Nothing ages like happiness.

An Ideal Husband

A man who allows himself to be convinced by an argument is a thoroughly unreasonable person.

An Ideal Husband

Nothing annoys people so much as not receiving invitations.

The Importance of Being Earnest

The emotions of man are stirred more quickly than man's intelligence—it is much more easy to have sympathy with suffering than it is to have sympathy with thought.

The Soul of Man Under Socialism

It isn't easy to be anything nowadays. There's such a lot of beastly competition about.

The Importance of Being Earnest

Three addresses always inspire confidence, even among tradesmen.

The Importance of Being Earnest

The public are all morbid, because the public can never find expression for anything.

The Soul of Man Under Socialism

Hesitation of any kind is a sign of mental decay in the young, of physical weakness in the old.

The Importance of Being Earnest

Wisdom comes with winters.

A Florentine Tragedy

It is always nice to be expected, and not to arrive.

An Ideal Husband

Personal experience is a most vicious and limited circle.

The Decay of Lying

To be premature is to be perfect.

Phrases and Philosophies for the Use of the Young

I have discovered that alcohol taken in sufficient quantity produces all the effects of drunkenness.

OSCAR WILDE

When we are happy we are always good, but when we are good we are not always happy.

OSCAR WILDE

Optimism

If you pretend to be good, the world takes you very seriously. If you pretend to be bad, it doesn't. Such is the astounding stupidity of optimism.

Lady Windermere's Fan

Paradigm

I find it harder and harder every day to live up to my blue china.

Oscar Wilde

This suspense is terrible. I hope it will last.

The Importance of Being Earnest

People who count their chickens before they are hatched, act very wisely, because chickens run about so absurdly that it is impossible to count them accurately.

Oscar Wilde

Cigarettes have at least the charm of leaving one unsatisfied.

The Critic as Artist

Between them Hugo and Shakespeare have exhausted every subject. Originality is no longer possible, even in sin. So there are no real emotions left, only extraordinary adjectives.

Oscar Wilde

If you are not too long, I will wait here for you all my life.

The Importance of Being Earnest

Politics

Wherever there is a man who exercises authority, there is a man who resists authority.

The Soul of Man Under Socialism

Discontent is the first step in the progress of a man or a nation.

A Woman of No Importance

One should never take sides in anything. Taking sides is the beginning of sincerity, and earnestness follows shortly afterwards, and the human being becomes a bore.

A Woman of No Importance

All modes of government are failures. Despotism is unjust to everybody, including the despot, who is probably made for better things. Oligarchies are unjust to the many, and ochlocracies are unjust to the few. High hopes were once formed of democracy; but democracy means simply the bludgeoning of the people by the people for the people. It has been found out.

The Soul of Man Under Socialism

If there was less sympathy in the world there would be less trouble in the world.

An Ideal Husband

In art, as in politics, grandfathers are always wrong *(les grandpères ont toujours tort)*.

The Picture of Dorian Gray

When Liberty comes with hands dabbled in blood, it is hard to shake hands with her.

OSCAR WILDE

To sweep a slushy crossing for eight hours on a day when the east wind is blowing is a disgusting occupation. To sweep it with mental, moral, or physical dignity seems to me to be impossible. To sweep it with joy would be appalling. Man is made for something better than disturbing dirt.

The Soul of Man Under Socialism

The idle grow eloquent over the dignity of labor.

OSCAR WILDE

It is well for our vanity that we slay the criminal, for if we suffered him to live he might show us what we had gained by his crime.

The Critic as Artist

Agitators are a set of interfering, meddling people, who come down to some perfectly contented class of the community, and sow the seeds of discontent amongst them. That is the reason why agitators are so absolutely necessary. Without them, in our incomplete state, there would be no advance towards civilization.

The Soul of Man Under Socialism

A regicide has always a place in history.

Vera, or The Nihilists

The less punishment, the less crime.

The Soul of Man Under Socialism

There is always more brass than brains in an aristocracy.

Vera, or The Nihilists

The Pope

I was deeply impressed, and my walking stick showed signs of budding.

OSCAR WILDE

Poverty

Charity creates a multitude of sins.

The Soul of Man Under Socialism

As for begging, it is safer to beg than to take, but it is finer to take than to beg.

The Soul of Man Under Socialism

They try to solve the problem of poverty, for instance, by keeping the poor alive; or, in the case of a very advanced school, by amusing the poor.

The Soul of Man Under Socialism

If the poor only had profiles there would be no difficulty in solving the problem of poverty.

Phrases and Philosophies for the Use of the Young

We are often told that the poor are grateful for charity. Some of them are, no doubt, but the best amongst the poor are never grateful. They are ungrateful, discontented, disobedient, and rebellious. They are quite right to be so. Charity they feel to be a ridiculously inadequate mode of partial restitution, or a sentimental dole, usually accompanied by some impertinent attempt on the part of the sentimentalist to tyrannize over their private lives. Why should they be grateful for the crumbs that fall from the rich man's table?

The Soul of Man Under Socialism

I am not at all in favor of amusements for the poor. Blankets and coals are sufficient.

A Woman of No Importance

The man who is poor is in himself absolutely of no importance. He is merely the infinitesimal atom of a force that, so far from regarding him, crushes him: indeed, prefers him crushed, as in that case he is far more obedient.

The Soul of Man Under Socialism

If I hadn't my debts I shouldn't have anything to think about.

A Woman of No Importance

Sometimes the poor are praised for being thrifty. But to recommend thrift to the poor is both grotesque and insulting. It is like advising a man who is starving to eat less. Man should not be ready to show that he can live like a badly fed animal.

The Soul of Man Under Socialism

The majority of people spoil their lives by an unhealthy and exaggerated altruism—are forced, indeed, so to spoil them.

The Soul of Man Under Socialism

As for the virtuous poor, one can pity them, of course, but one cannot possibly admire them. They have made private terms with the enemy, and sold their birthright for very bad pottage. They must also be extraordinarily stupid.

The Soul of Man Under Socialism

Misery and poverty are so absolutely degrading, and exercise such a paralyzing effect over the nature of men, that no class is ever really conscious of its own suffering. They have to be told of it by other people, and they often entirely disbelieve them.

The Soul of Man Under Socialism

There is only one class in the community that thinks more about money than the rich, and that is the poor. The poor can think of nothing else. That is the misery of being poor.

The Soul of Man Under Socialism

The only thing that can console one for being poor is extravagance. The only thing that can console one for being rich is economy.

OSCAR WILDE

The Press

In the old days men had the rack. Now they have the Press.

The Soul of Man Under Socialism

As for modern journalism, it is not my business to defend it. It justifies its own existence by the great Darwinian principle of the survival of the vulgarest.

The Critic as Artist

It is only the unreadable that occurs.

A Woman of No Importance

He must be quite respectable. One has never heard his name before in the whole course of one's life, which speaks volumes for a man, nowadays.

A Woman of No Importance

If you survive yellow journalism you need not be afraid of yellow fever.

Oscar Wilde

In centuries before ours the public nailed the ears of journalists to the pump. That was quite hideous. In this century journalists have nailed their own ears to keyholes.

The Soul of Man Under Socialism

It was a fatal day when the public discovered that the pen is mightier than the paving-stone, and can be made as offensive as the brickbat. They at once sought for the journalist, found him, developed him, and made him their industrious and well-paid servant. It is greatly to be regretted, for both their sakes. Behind the barricade there may be much that is noble and heroic. But what is there behind the leading-article but prejudice, stupidity, cant and twaddle? And when these four are joined together they make a terrible force, and constitute the new authority.

The Soul of Man Under Socialism

Progress

A map of the world that does not include Utopia is not worth even glancing at, for it leaves out the one country at which Humanity is always landing. And when Humanity lands there, it looks out, and, seeing a better country, sets sail. Progress is the realization of Utopias.

The Soul of Man Under Socialism

Religion

I remember having read somewhere, in some strange book, that when the gods wish to punish us they answer our prayers.

An Ideal Husband

Religions die when they are proved to be true. Science is the record of dead religions.

Phrases and Philosophies for the Use of the Young

I have never been shocked in my life. I think to be shocked by anything shows a very low ethical standard. Nobody is ever shocked now-a-days except the clergy and the middle classes. It is the profession of the one and the punishment of the other.

The Importance of Being Earnest

I don't mind plain women being Puritans. It is the only excuse they have for being plain.

A Woman of No Importance

We live, as I hope you know, in an age of ideals. The fact is constantly mentioned in the more expensive monthly magazines, and has reached the provincial pulpits, I am told.

The Importance of Being Earnest

It is well for his peace that the saint goes to his martyrdom. He is spared the sight of the horror of his harvest.

The Critic as Artist

To be either a Puritan, a prig or a preacher is a bad thing. To be all three at once reminds me of the worst excesses of the French Revolution.

Oscar Wilde

Those who see any difference between soul and body have neither.

Phrases and Philosophies for the Use of the Young

Surely providence can resist temptation by this time.

Lord Arthur Savile's Crime

She was positively violent. I never heard such language in the whole course of my life from anyone. She might just as well have been in a pulpit. I shouldn't be at all surprised if she took to philanthropy or something of the sort and abused her fellow creatures for the rest of her life.

The Importance of Being Earnest

Where will it all end? Half the world does not believe in God, and the other half does not believe in me.

OSCAR WILDE

Prayer must never be answered. If it is, it ceases to be prayer and becomes correspondence.

OSCAR WILDE

Heaven is a despotism. I shall be at home there.

Vera, or The Nihilists

Russia

A Russian who lives happily under the present system of government in Russia must either believe that man has no soul, or that, if he has, it is not worth developing.

Oscar Wilde

Self

I could deny myself the pleasure of talking, but not to others the pleasure of listening.

OSCAR WILDE

I am the only person in the world I should like to know thoroughly.

Lady Windermere's Fan

To love oneself is the beginning of a lifelong romance.

Phrases and Philosophies for the Use of the Young

Duty is what one expects from others, it is not what one does oneself.

A Woman of No Importance

My weakness is that I do what I will and get what I want.

OSCAR WILDE

God save me from my disciples.

OSCAR WILDE

I am always astonishing myself. It is the only thing that
makes life worth living.

A Woman of No Importance

I like to do all the talking myself. It saves time and
prevents arguments.

The Remarkable Rocket

I never travel without my diary.
One should always have
something sensational to read in
the train.

The Importance of Being Earnest

I don't at all like knowing what people say of me behind
my back. It makes me far too conceited.

An Ideal Husband

What is a selfish person? A selfish person is surely one
who seeks to keep his joys and sorrows to himself.

The Importance of Being Earnest

Even the disciple has his uses. He stands behind one's throne, and at the moment of one's triumph whispers in one's ear that, after all, one is immortal.

OSCAR WILDE

Only one thing remains infinitely fascinating to me, the mystery of moods. To be master of these moods is exquisite, to be mastered by them more exquisite still.

OSCAR WILDE

Shallowness

I hate people who are not serious about meals. It is so shallow of them.

The Importance of Being Earnest

Only the shallow know themselves.

Phrases and Philosophies for the Use of the Young

It is only the shallow people who do not judge by appearances.

Oscar Wilde

It is only the superficial qualities that last. Man's deeper nature is soon found out.

Phrases and Philosophies for the Use of the Young

Slavery

The fact is, that civilization requires slaves. The Greeks were quite right there. Unless there are slaves to do the ugly, horrible, uninteresting work, culture and contemplation become almost impossible. Human slavery is wrong, insecure and demoralizing. On mechanical slavery, on the slavery of the machine, the future of the world depends.

The Soul of Man Under Socialism

It is clear, then, that no Authoritarian Socialism will do. For while under the present system a very large number of people can lead lives of a certain amount of freedom and expression and happiness, under an industrial-barrack system, or a system of economic tyranny, nobody would be able to have any such freedom at all. It is to be regretted that a portion of our community should be practically in slavery, but to propose to solve the problem by enslaving the entire community is childish.

The Soul of Man Under Socialism

$\mathcal{N}$ever speak disrespectfully of Society. Only people who can't get into it do that.

The Importance of Being Earnest

Talk to every woman as if you loved her, and to every man as if he bored you, and at the end of your first season you will have the reputation of possessing the most perfect social tact.

A Woman of No Importance

Spade

I would like to protest against the statement that I have ever called a spade a spade. The man who did so should be condemned to use one.

OSCAR WILDE

Style

In all unimportant matters, style, not sincerity, is the essential. In all important matters, style, not sincerity, is the essential.

*Phrases and Philosophies for
the Use of the Young*

I want a natural style, with a touch of affectation.

Oscar Wilde

Only the great masters of style ever succeed in being obscure.

*Phrases and Philosophies for
the Use of the Young*

There are distinct social possibilities in your profile. The two weak points in our age are its want of principle and its want of profile. The chin a little higher, dear. Style largely depends on the way the chin is worn. They are worn very high, just at present.

The Importance of Being Earnest

When one pays a visit, it is for the purpose of wasting other people's time, not one's own.

An Ideal Husband

The amount of pleasure one gets out of dialect is a matter entirely of temperament. To say "mither" instead of "mother" seems to many the acme of romance. There are others who are not quite so ready to believe in the pathos of provincialism.

OSCAR WILDE

Theater

It is a humiliating confession, but we are all of us made out of the same stuff. In Falstaff there is something of Hamlet, in Hamlet there is not a little of Falstaff.

The Decay of Lying

Ordinary women never appeal to one's imagination. They are limited to their century. No glamour ever transfigures them. One knows their minds as easily as one knows their bonnets. One can always find them. There is no mystery in any of them. They ride in the Park in the morning, and chatter at tea-parties in the afternoon. They have their stereotyped smile, and their fashionable manner. They are quite obvious. But an actress! How different an actress is!

The Picture of Dorian Gray

Actors are so fortunate. They can choose whether they will appear in tragedy or in comedy, whether they will suffer or make merry, laugh or shed tears. But in real life it is different. Most men and women are forced to perform parts for which they have no qualifications. Our Guildensterns play Hamlet for us and our Hamlets have to jest like Prince Hal. The world is a stage, but the play is badly cast.

Lord Arthur Savile's Crime

Truth

My experience of life is that whenever one tells a lie one is corroborated on every side. When one tells the truth one is left in a very lonely and painful position, and no one believes a word one says.

The Importance of Being Earnest

Many a young man starts in life with a natural gift for exaggeration which, if nurtured in congenial and sympathetic surroundings, or by the imitation of the best models, might grow into something really great and wonderful. But, as a rule, he comes to nothing. He either falls into careless habits of accuracy, or takes to frequenting the society of the aged and well-informed.

The Decay of Lying

If one tells the truth, one is sure, sooner or later, to be found out.

Phrases and Philosophies for the Use of the Young

It is perfectly monstrous the way people go about, nowadays, saying things against one behind one's back that are absolutely and entirely truth.

A Woman of No Importance

A thing is not necessarily true because a man dies for it.

The Portrait of Mr. W.H.

Lying for the sake of the improvement of the young, which is the basis of home education, still lingers amongst us, and its advantages are so admirably set forth in the early books of Plato's *Republic* that it is unnecessary to dwell upon them here.

The Decay of Lying

There was a great deal of truth, I dare say, in what you said, and you looked very pretty while you said it, which is much more important.

A Woman of No Importance

Upon the other hand, to corroborate a lie is a distinctly cowardly action. I know it is a thing that the newspapers do one for the other, every day. But it is not the act of a gentleman. No gentleman ever corroborates a thing that he knows to be untrue.

The Importance of Being Earnest

After all, what is a fine lie? Simply that which is its own evidence. If a man is sufficiently unimaginative to produce evidence in support of a lie, he might just as well speak the truth all at once.

The Decay of Lying

There is such a thing as robbing a story of its reality by trying to make it too true.

The Decay of Lying

For the aim of the liar is simply to charm, to delight, to give pleasure. He is the very basis of civilized society, and without him a dinner-party, even at the mansions of the great, is as dull as a lecture.

The Decay of Lying

I will tell you, if you solemnly promise to tell everybody else.

A Woman of No Importance

When a truth becomes a fact it loses all its intellectual value.

OSCAR WILDE

A truth ceases to be true when more than one person believes in it.

Phrases and Philosophies for the Use of the Young

Two Sorts

It is absurd to divide people into good and bad. People are either charming or tedious.

Lady Windermere's Fan

Where the cultured catch an effect, the uncultured catch cold.

The Decay of Lying

There are only two kinds of women, the plain and the colored. The plain women are very useful. If you want to gain a reputation for respectability, you have merely to take them down to supper. The other women are very charming. They commit one mistake, however. They paint in order to try and look young. Our grandmothers painted in order to try and talk brilliantly. *Rouge* and esprit used to go together. That is all over now. As long as a woman can look ten years younger than her own daughter, she is perfectly satisfied.

The Picture of Dorian Gray

Women are never disarmed by compliments. Men always are. That is the difference between the two sexes.

An Ideal Husband

In this world there are only two tragedies. One is not getting what one wants, and the other is getting it.

Lady Windermere's Fan

The well-bred contradict other people. The wise contradict themselves.

Phrases and Philosophies for the Use of the Young

Vulgarity

It is very vulgar to talk about one's business. Only people like stockbrokers do that, and then merely at dinner parties.

The Importance of Being Earnest

Vulgarity is simply the conduct of other people.

An Ideal Husband

I dislike arguments of any kind. They are always vulgar, and often convincing.

The Importance of Being Earnest

Vulgarity and stupidity are two very vivid facts in modern life. One regrets them, naturally. But there they are. They are subjects for study, like everything else.

The Soul of Man Under Socialism

No crime is vulgar, but all vulgarity is crime.

Phrases and Philosophies for the Use of the Young

Vulgar habit that is people have nowadays of asking one, after one has given them an idea, whether one is serious or not. Nothing is serious except passion.

A Woman of No Importance

As long as war is regarded as wicked it will always have its fascination. When it is looked upon as vulgar, it will cease to be popular.

OSCAR WILDE

Wagner

Only relatives, or creditors, ever ring in that Wagnerian manner.

The Importance of Being Earnest

I like Wagner so much better than other composers, because he is so loud that one can talk the whole time without the risk of being overheard.

OSCAR WILDE

Weather

𝒲henever people talk to me about the weather, I always feel quite certain that they mean something else.

The Importance of Being Earnest

Wickedness

Wicked women bother one. Good women bore one. That is the only difference between them.

Lady Windermere's Fan

Wickedness is a myth invented by good people to account for the curious attractiveness of others.

Phrases and Philosophies for the Use of the Young

Women

One should never trust a woman who tells one her real age. A woman who would tell one that, would tell one anything.

A Woman of No Importance

Crying is the refuge of plain women but the ruin of pretty ones.

Lady Windermere's Fan

We women adore failures. They lean on us.

A Woman of No Importance

Women are a fascinatingly willful sex. Every woman is a rebel, and usually in wild revolt against herself.

A Woman of No Importance

You are perfectly right in making some slight alteration. Indeed, no woman should ever be quite accurate about her age. It looks so calculating.

The Importance of Being Earnest

It is every woman's duty never to leave men alone for a single moment, except during this short breathing space after dinner; without which, I believe, we poor women would be absolutely worn to shadows.

A Woman of No Importance

Girls never marry the men they flirt with. Girls don't think it right.

The Importance of Being Earnest

Women are pictures. Men are problems. If you want to know what a woman really means—which, by the way is always a dangerous thing to do—look at her, don't listen to her.

A Woman of No Importance

Sphinxes without secrets.

A Woman of No Importance

The history of women is the history of the worst form of
tyranny the world has ever known. The tyranny of the
weak over the strong. It is the only tyranny that lasts.

A Woman of No Importance

I don't quite like women who are interested in
philanthropic work. I think it is so forward of them.

The Importance of Being Earnest

Thirty-five is a very attractive age. Society is full of
women of the very highest birth who have, of their own
free choice, remained thirty-five for years.

The Importance of Being Earnest

If a woman really repents, she has to go to a bad
dressmaker, otherwise no one believes in her.

Lady Windermere's Fan

Women never know when the curtain has fallen. They
always want a sixth act, and as soon as the interest of the
play is entirely over, they propose to continue it.

Oscar Wilde

How absurd to talk of the equality of the sexes! Where questions of self-sacrifice are concerned, men are infinitely beyond us.

The Importance of Being Earnest

Youth

The old believe every-thing: the middle-aged suspect everything: the young know everything.

Phrases and Philosophies for the Use of the Young

Those whom the gods love grow young.

<small>OSCAR WILDE</small>

The youth of the present day are quite monstrous. They have absolutely no respect for dyed hair.

Lady Windermere's Fan

The condition of perfection is idleness: the aim of perfection is youth.

Phrases and Philosophies for the Use of the Young

There is nothing like youth. The middle-aged are mortgaged to Life. The old are in life's lumber room. But youth is the Lord of Life. Youth has a kingdom waiting for it. Every one is born a king, and most people die in exile, like most kings. To win back my youth, there is nothing I wouldn't do—except take exercise, get up early, or be a useful member of the community.

A Woman of No Importance

The old-fashioned respect for the young is fast dying out.

The Importance of Being Earnest

The soul is born old but grows young. That is the comedy of life. And the body is born young and grows old. That is life's tragedy.

A Woman of No Importance

John Calvin Batchelor is the author of eight books, including his most recent novel, *Father's Day*. He lives with his wife, son, and daughter in New York City.

Craig McNeer is a writer who lives in New York City.